A MASK FOR JANUS

Yale Series of Younger Poets · Volume 49

edited by W. H. Auden

Published on the Mary Cady Tew Memorial Fund

A MASK FOR JANUS

by W. S. MERWIN

with a Foreword by W. H. Auden

New Haven : Yale University Press

Centenary Edition, 2019

Published with assistance from a grant to honor James Merrill.
Originally published in 1952 by Yale University Press with
assistance from the Mary Cady Tew Memorial Fund.

Library of Congress Catalog Card Number: 52–5355
ISBN 978-0-300-24638-4 (paperback : alk. paper)

A catalogue record for this book is
available from the British Library.

Certain of these poems have previously appeared or
been accepted for publication in the following peri-
odicals: in the United States in *Furioso*, *The Hudson Review*,
The Kenyon Review, *Western Review*, *Poetry: A Magazine of
Verse*, *The Quarterly Review of Literature*; and in England
in *The Times Literary Supplement*, *The Listener*, *Poetry* (*London*),
Nine, *Poetry Quarterly*, *Poetry: Quarterly Magazine*, *Mandrake*,
and *New Poems Anthology* (Michael Joseph Ltd.).

This paper meets the requirements of ANSI/NISO
Z39.48-1992 (Permanence of Paper).

Yale University Press books may be purchased in
quantity for educational, business, or promotional use.
For information, please e-mail sales.press@yale.edu
(U.S. office) or sales@yaleup.co.uk (U.K. office).

10 9 8 7 6 5 4 3 2 1

FOR DOROTHY

Habit is evil, all habit, even speech,
And promises prefigure their own breech.

JOHN HALL WHEELOCK

. . . pone cara de mia . . .

PEDRO SALINAS

FOREWORD

IN EVERY SUCCESSFUL POEM *the reader encounters,
at one and the same time, a historically unique experience—
what occurs in the poem has occurred for the first and last time—
and an experience which is universally significant—analogous
experiences have always occurred and will continue to occur to
all men. In respect of these two elements, most poems fall into
one of two classes, those in which the historic occasion is, so to
speak, on the outside and the general significance on the inside,
and those in which their positions are the other way round. In
the first kind of poem, the overt subject of the poem is a specific
experience undergone by the "I" of the poem at a specific time
and place—whether the experience actually occurred to the poet
or was invented makes no difference—and the universal
significance is implied, not stated directly. In the second kind,
the overt subject is universal and impersonal, frequently a myth,
and it is the personal experience of the poet which is implied.
Most of the poems of Robert Frost belong to the first category,
those of Paul Valéry to the second, while Yeats alternates
between writing "occasional" and "mythological" poetry.*

*Neither kind, of course, is better or greater than the other,
but each has its peculiar danger. In uninspired hands, the
occasional approach degenerates into triviality and journalism—
the occasion described is without significant resonance—while
the mythological approach becomes "literary" in the bad sense,*

a mere elegant manifestation of the imaginative work of the dead without any live relation to the present of the writer or his reader.

Silly and tiresome as is that favorite question of reporters, "What are the trends in poetry today?" it is impossible, if one compares a contemporary issue of any literary magazine with an issue of fifteen years back, not to recognize certain changes in content, and among these the most obvious is the increase of interest shown today, both by poets and critics, in myth, and a corresponding turning away, on the part of the poets at least, from occasional subjects whether political or private.

The shift of concern is probably a fortunate one, particularly for a young poet, like Mr. Merwin. To be able to speak in one's own person and directly in terms of one's own experience without making a fool of oneself requires a wisdom and assumed authority which is more likely to come, if it comes at all, in later life, but the profundity and eternal relevance to the human condition of the great myths cannot fail to instill the most immature writer who reflects upon them with that reverence and wonder without which no man can become wise.

One of Mr. Merwin's best poems, "Dictum: For a Masque of Deluge," is based upon the myth of the Flood. The historical experience which is latent in the poem is, I fancy, the feeling which most of us share of being witnesses to the collapse of a civilization, a collapse which transcends all political differences and for which we are all collectively responsible, and in addition feeling that this collapse is not final but that, on the other side of disaster, there will be some kind of rebirth, though we cannot imagine its nature. By translating these feelings into mythical terms, the poet is able to avoid what a direct

viii

*treatment could scarcely have avoided, namely, the use of names
and events which will probably turn out not to have been
the really significant ones.*

*With his concern for the traditional conceptions of Western
culture as expressed in its myths, Mr. Merwin combines
an admirable respect for its traditions of poetic craftsmanship.
His carols show how carefully he has studied Spanish
versification, and in poems like "For a Dissolving Music"
and "A Dance of Death" he has not been ashamed to write
what are frankly technical exercises. Apart from the fact
that works which set out to be exercises in technique often end
by being works of art as well, e.g. the Chopin Etudes, the
mastery of his medium through diligent practice is of
incalculable value to any artist. Technique in itself cannot make
a good poem, but the lack of it can spoil one. The final stanza
of "Dictum" shows the reward that Mr. Merwin has earned
by his studies.*

> *A falling frond may seem all trees. If so
> We know the tone of falling. We shall find
> Dictions for rising, words for departure;
> And time will be sufficient before that revel
> To teach an order and rehearse the days
> Till the days are accomplished: so now the dove
> Makes assignations with the olive tree,
> Slurs with her voice the gestures of the time:
> The day foundering, the dropping sun
> Heavy, the wind a low portent of rain.*

*No one who had not previously trained himself thoroughly in
the mechanics of verse could have varied so skillfully the position*

of the caesura from line to line, a variation on which so much of the poetic effect depends.

In conclusion, reflecting upon the general tenor of Mr. Merwin's poetry as an example of the younger generations of American poets, I am reminded of a remarkable prophecy in de Tocqueville's Democracy in America *concerning the poetry of the future. Of its accuracy I must leave the reader to judge.*

> *When skepticism had depopulated heaven . . . the poets . . . turned their eyes to inanimate Nature. As they lost sight of Gods and heroes, they set themselves to describe streams and mountains. . . . Some have thought this . . . the kind of poetry peculiar to democratic ages; but I believe it only belongs to a period of transition.*
>
> *I am persuaded that in the end democracy diverts the imagination from all that is external to man, and fixes it on man alone. . . .*
>
> *. . . [The] poets living in democratic ages will prefer the delineation of passions and ideas to that of persons and achievements. The language, the dress, and the daily actions of men in democracies are repugnant to ideal conceptions. . . . This forces the poet constantly to search below the external surface which is palpable to the senses, in order to read the inner soul. . . .*
>
> *. . . The destinies of mankind—man himself, taken aloof from his age and his country, and standing in the presence of Nature and of God, with his passions,*

his doubts, his rare prosperities, and inconceivable wretchedness—will become the chief, if not the sole theme of poetry among these nations.*

W. H. Auden

**Alexis de Tocqueville*, Democracy in America, *tr. Henry Reeve,* ed. Henry Steele Commager (New York, Oxford University Press, 1947), pp. 290–294.

CONTENTS

ANABASIS

(I)

Then we poised, in time's fullness brought
As to a new country, the senses
In the mutations of a sallow light,
A season of signs and speechless;

Thought momently on nothing, knew
No oratory, no welcome:
Silence about our silence grew;
Beached by the convenient stream.

Night is familiar when it comes.
On dim gestures does the mind
Exorcise abandoned limbs,
Disbodied, of that other land

Estranged almost beyond response,
A bleached and faintly relevant
Signature to stir the sense
In veteran usage and intent.

One dreams fixed beasts that drowse or wonder,
Not blinking; by the stream a few
Poplars and white beeches where
Exhausted leaves, suspended, through

The distant autumn do not fall,
Or, fallen, fired, are unconsumed,
The flame perduring, the still
Smoke eternal in the mind.

(Embarrassed, these scarred penates
Smile, between raw stones supported,
Musing perhaps an anomalous
Speech no longer understood.)

We ponder, after damp sundown,
The slow boats departing, heavy,
In another time; our direction
Moved in the cool rain away:

We with brief knowledge hazarded
Alien influence and tropic,
Entered and did diversely thread
What degradations, false music,

Straits whose rocks lean to the sound,
Monstrous, of their declivities,
As lovers on their private ground
See no distance, but face and face;

We have passed in a warm light
Islands whose charmed habitants
Doze on the shores to dissipate
The seasons of their indolence;

Even against those borders led
Lapped by the forgetful rivers
Have stood among the actual dead,
No breath moving the gray flowers.

The remnant of all passage lies
Cold or distorted in the brain
As tall fables of strangers, as
Lisped visions of other men.

(The neighbor waters flame and wave:
All that we could not bring away
Our hands, as though with courage, have
Burned, and the tired ships where they lay.)

The covenant we could but seize
Fractionally by the ear
And dreamed it substance, that the eyes
Might follow—and its motions were

3

Hands that toy about a door
In dreams and melt where they caress,
Not displacing the wind they wear—
Brought us to this final place.

We see the various brain enclosed
Never the promise, but its guise:
Terrain in private we supposed
That always in its Easter is.

Rather, in priestly winter bide
Our shadows where no prayers will work
That unison we faintly, toward
Our time and litany, invoke.

You, satisfied under no sky,
Even from this air your air is fled,
Your singular authority
Vain, no richness where you bled,

But you are dwindled and now die
To a vexed but promissory shape
For an old man stroked always by
The vague extremities of sleep:

So were he tangled to believe,
By euphory and the leaves' dictions.
His grave members did walk and weave,
Blessed, among the many mansions.

4

ANABASIS
(II)

After the first night and bare morning passed
We remembered the gray wings of a gull
That traced us seaward when our eyes had lost
The thread of last whiteness where the land fell.

After the first days, one when the world turned
Dark and the rain came, we remembered fires
In lost houses; we stared and lurched half-blind
Against new darkness, neither night's nor ours.

We survived the selves that we remembered;
We have dozed on gradual seas where slowly
The hours changed on the silence, and a word,
Falling, expired in the sufficient day.

Sometimes through a mirage or evening rose
Towers where the myths sleep and the lanterns;
We fled a saeculum what sick repose,
But woke at morning where the fever burned.

We have slid on a seizure of the wind
To spume-blindness where our fear became
A whirling without chronicle or end;
There we circled and bent the thought of time

Till, saved by violence from violence,
We, the gesture of rages not our own,
Forsook and followed, motion without sense,
Where we were drawn, from pool and tempest thrown.

In wake of storms we came where the gulls cry
Allusions to dim archipelagoes;
We coaxed our souls and sembled where we lay
The last exhaustion, as the buzzard knows.

We had seen strengths flee or degenerate:
Even the wind starved in our tracks and died,
Till, on that mirror, we, the image, thought,
After the petrel-, of the halcyon-dead.

Thus calmed we lay and hungered east or west
But drifted on what warm meridian,
Grazing the reefs of dying; yet we passed
Through that peripety and afternoon.

6

We saw the islands of a new season.
We were made young with watching, and our eyes
Believed a garden and reserve where swung
The fruits that from all hungers immunize.

There when we called, the startled land returned
A precipitate waking as of a child;
Our vision built on the approaching sand;
We entered channels where the coral smiled,

And but the countries of occasion found:
There at sundown, lodged where the tide lingers,
Among the driftwood and the casual drowned,
Slept on the lulled questions of those rivers.

We have half-waked to hear the minutes die
And heard our minds that, waiting toward the east,
Embraced the seed and thought of day, and we
Were by the pool of dark the crouchèd beast.

But not the watchers of unheard-of shores
Know to repeat our prayers when we became
The eyes of sleep that chased receding fires
Through the bodiless exile of a dream.

Between sleep and the vacant excellence
Of seas we suffered music that declares
The monstrous fixities of innocence;
We are children of a different curse.

In dream there was no answer nor command,
Yet there did rumors beyond reason sway
Waters that slipped from an escaping land
All night, and we are tidal and obey.

We were already far when morning died.
We watched the colors sink, and all the light.
We turned from silence and fearfully made
Our small language in the place of night.

In fear of the swift bird that shouts and sees
In these tides and dark entrails the curled
Augurs of unreasonable seas
We seek a new dimension for the world.

But sentenced are the seasons that we know.
The serpent holds and the whirlwind harries
The last oceans where the drowned pursue
The daze and fall of fabulous voyages.

Still we are strange to orisons and knees.
Fixed to bone only, foreign as we came,
We float leeward till the mind and body lose
The uncertain continent of a name.

8

RIME OF
THE PALMERS

Where, and in the morning,
Palmers, do you pass?
The sudden birds sing
In the poplar trees.

Where, and away from morning,
Palmers, do you follow,
And where are you going
That you take no shadow,

And what carry, stranger,
That no shadow take?
—Hunger is sleeping where
Staff and shadow break.

9

Bone and vein are full
Where we sat at meat;
We seek the still
Wonder that we eat.

Our motion is our form
And our passage raiment;
Between stillness and time
We pass, improvident.

—Form is a thing goes slyly
And escapes our ears;
In another country
What did you love, palmers,

And what do you remember
This morning and light?
—We go (may wonder
Send and receive our feet)

Half-remembering
Where our bones were hid
And the wind at evening
There where hunger died,

And the evening wind
That everywhere and sorely
Turned and complained
As we came away.

—The wind is at morning
On the high meadow;
What are you singing,
Palmers, as you go,

And what do your lips say
When I hear no sound?
—Speech is a thorny way
In a hard land,

And into absence,
Into quiet goes:
Before the silence,
After the voice,

We sing, and without words,
An air of promise,
As the waking birds
In the poplar trees.

—The last stars show
On the chill season;
You start betimes, you go,
Palmers, in night and dawn:

You move to what increase,
Neither night's nor day's?
—The winds disposing peace
There where our vision is;

But, moving, shall we say
We are fire or storm,
Or as one that, wholly
Name, or without a name,

Comes, or has appeared,
Or the voice thereafter?
Who knows the word
That we are carol for?

—A word is a little thing,
And the letter kills,
And you are far who sing
From the morning hills,

And what is the high road,
And the road where you go?
—We have been the dead
And what the dead know:

At the broken bridge
Where the cold rivers
Move in a rage,
Let the breath be prayers;

If music speak softly
Forget what it tells
Where you go blind and high
By the wild hills;

At the nighted gates
By the last mountain
There age forgets
And the child is slain:

If hope bring you there
Where night's self darkly burns,
Abandon hope to air
And to the wind's returns;

If a dim leaf tremble
And then the dawn come back,
Oh, begin carols
By that morning lake.

—But pleasure discovers
By what sense and lights,
Bridge and hills, palmers,
And the nighted gates?

But you leave us. Afterward
What shall we say, palmers?
Say: the birds suddenly
Sing in the poplar trees.

That the word was morning once
That is common day;
In mention of our bones,
Of our bodies say:

Rain is a perilous friend,
The sweet wind blows foreign;
These pictures made of mind
And these hungers gone

And these palmers that on
A field of summer went
Are perfect and lie down
Thus, lest the land repent.

BALLAD OF JOHN CABLE
AND THREE GENTLEMEN

He that had come that morning,
One after the other,
Over seven hills,
Each of a new color,

Came now by the last tree,
By the red-colored valley,
To a gray river
Wide as the sea.

There at the shingle
A listing wherry
Awash with dark water;
What should it carry?

There on the shelving,
Three dark gentlemen.
Might they direct him?
Three gentlemen.

"Cable, friend John, John Cable,"
When they saw him they said,
"Come and be company
As far as the far side."

"Come follow the feet," they said,
"Of your family,
Of your old father
That came already this way."

But Cable said, "First I must go
Once to my sister again;
What will she do come spring
And no man on her garden?

She will say 'Weeds are alive
From here to the Stream of Friday;
I grieve for my brother's plowing,'
Then break and cry."

"Lose no sleep," they said, "for that fallow:
She will say before summer,
'I can get me a daylong man,
Do better than a brother.' "

Cable said, "I think of my wife:
Dearly she needs consoling;
I must go back for a little
For fear she die of grieving."

"Cable," they said, "John Cable,
Ask no such wild favor;
Still, if you fear she die soon,
The boat might wait for her."

But Cable said, "I remember:
Out of charity let me
Go shore up my poorly mother,
Cries all afternoon."

They said, "She is old and far,
Far and rheumy with years,
And, if you like, we shall take
No note of her tears."

But Cable said, "I am neither
Your hired man nor maid,
Your dog nor shadow
Nor your ape to be led."

He said, "I must go back:
Once I heard someone say
That the hollow Stream of Friday
Is a rank place to lie;

And this word, now I remember,
Makes me sorry: have you
Thought of my own body
I was always good to?

The frame that was my devotion
And my blessing was,
The straight bole whose limbs
Were long as stories—

Now, poor thing, left in the dirt
By the Stream of Friday
Might not remember me
Half tenderly."

They let him nurse no worry;
They said, "We give you our word:
Poor thing is made of patience;
Will not say a word."

"Cable, friend John, John Cable,"
After this they said,
"Come with no company
To the far side.

To a populous place,
A dense city
That shall not be changed
Before much sorrow dry."

Over shaking water
Toward the feet of his father,
Leaving the hills' color
And his poorly mother

And his wife at grieving
And his sister's fallow
And his body lying
In the rank hollow,

Now Cable is carried
On the dark river;
Not even a shadow
Followed him over.

On the wide river
Gray as the sea
Flags of white water
Are his company.

MENG TZU'S SONG

The sparrows gleaning gutters
Kick and shuffle the horsehair,
And the simple wind that stirs
Their feathers stirs my hair.

How can I know, now forty
Years have shuffled my shoulders,
Whether my mind is steady
Or quakes as the wind stirs?

Because one sparrow, running
On the old wind-ruts, can be
Turned by an unseen thing,
A small wind in the sky,

And changes, it sets me thinking;
Yet I know not if my mind
Is moved, or is but sinking
Alone to its own kind.

If my mind moves not in wind
Or other breaths, it is not
Strange; at forty the mind
Of Kao Tzu wavered not.

Lo, how is the kept wind let
Out to make trouble with me!
How can one remain not
Moving before his eye?

One cultivates bravery
That the skin's hair not flinch
Nor the frail eye flee
Nor the blood blanch.

One is as the trodden inch
Of horsehair on the bare ground
At the market place: wrench
Nor kick wring from him sound.

Thinks he as though he were sand
Or horsehair, should the stiff sword
Shave the strength from his mind
And stab away his word.

Thinks of defeat and blood,
All hairs blown from control,
The hands like hair in mud
As though it mattered little.

How can the thin mind be able?
How put off quaking only,
Keeping all else simple,
Even in wind steady?

The wind is stiff and is high.
Simple the wind. The open
Coat of horsehair on three
Sides flaps without passion.

BLIND WILLIAM'S SONG

Stand from my shadow where it goes
Threaded upon a white dream,
From my clear eyes that take no light
And give no mercy.

I stood in clean Monday and heard
Seventy tongues of fire
Burn down from their talk.
I am the ash that walk.

Tuesday was dusty feet;
I shall not be the first
Who walked and did not know
The earth, the middle earth.

Wednesday, if it came,
I was a blown curse
And who are you not withered?
Tempt not my memory.

But though I was, on Thursday,
In that late morning,
Multiple as rain
And fell as rain falls

And have been on Friday
Say a white horse racing
—Since I see no motion
All speed is easy—

I have not been the sea
(My dry bone forbids me)
Whose blind repeated loss
Any loud tide will serve.

Lull the stones over me,
I that on Saturday
Closed about myself
And raged and was the grave.

Sunday I lie down
Within without my body;
All colored creation
Is tamed white by time.

FOR A DISSOLVING MUSIC

What shall be seen?
Limbs of a man
old and alone,
his shadow with him,
going and gone.
What shall be heard?
A hollow rime:
the heart gone tame
knocking afraid.
What shall be known?
Briefly the name,
but its frame shaken,
house of time
blown and broken,
draughty room,
dwindled flame,
red coal come
out of the warm,
dry honeycomb,
ended dream.

What shall be said?
This word if any:
time and blood
are spent money,
rain in a sieve;
summer is dead
(whom fools believe)
in a far grave,
worms receive
her fire to wive,
fear walks alive,
prayers I would weave,
pains I have,
hopes not many;
wherefore grieve
o splintered stave,
withered glove,
dry groove,
shaken sleeve
empty of love.

What shall be sung?
This song uneven:
eleven, seven,
chance cloven,
joints spavin,
blood chill-driven,
flesh craven,
breath not often,
teeth riven,
all day shriven,
last coven,
all night raven,
all doom woven,
none forgiven,
no curse ungraven,
no peace at even,
remnant for leaven,
promise true-given,
field but shaven,
nor hope of heaven.

HALF
ROUNDEL

I make no prayer
For the spoilt season,
The weed of Eden.
I make no prayer.
      Save us the green
      In the weed of time.

Now is November;
In night uneasy
Nothing I say.
I make no prayer.
      Save us from water
      That washes us away.

What do I ponder?
All smiled disguise,
Lights in cold places.
I make no prayer.
 Save us from air
 That wears us loosely.

The leaf of summer
To cold has come
In little time.
I make no prayer.
 From earth deliver
 And the dark therein.

Now is no whisper
Through all the living.
I speak to nothing.
I make no prayer.
 Save us from fire
 Consuming up and down.

King

I saw from a silk pillow
All high stations and low
Smile when I spoke, and bow,
And obey and follow.
All men do as I do.
I went in gold and yellow,
Ermine and gemmed shoe,
And was human even so,
Et, ecce, nunc in pulvere dormio.

Monk

I hoped that all sinners who
Wore a saintly sorrow
Into heaven should go.
All this did I do:
Walk with the eyes low,
Keep lonely pillow,
Many days go
Fasting and hollow,
All my bounty bestow,
Et, ecce, nunc in pulvere dormio.

Scholar

I sat like a shadow,
The light sallow,
Reasoning yes and no.
One thing I came to know.
I heard the mouse go,
Heard whispers in the tallow,
Wind disputing, "Although . . ."
Night on the candle blow,
Et, ecce, nunc in pulvere dormio.

Huntsman

The wind blew
In the cold furrow;
The falcon flew;
These did I follow:
Deerhound, doe,
Fox upon snow,
And sent the arrow,
And was chased, who did follow,
And came to this burrow,
Et, ecce, nunc in pulvere dormio.

Farmer

I walked with plow
On the green fallow;
All I did harrow
Dirt does undo.
Out at elbow
I lie to mellow,
Set in a furrow,
The weeds' fellow,
Quod, ecce, nunc in pulvere dormio.

Woman

I was as green willow,
My hands white and slow,
Love and increase below.
Be reaped as you did sow.
I am bitter as rue.
Now am I also
Defaced and hollow,
Nursing no shadow,
Quod, ecce, nunc in pulvere dormio.

Epitaph

Lords, I forget what I knew;
I saw false and true,
Sad and antic show,
Did profane and hallow,
Saw the worthies go
Into the still hollow
And wrote their words, even so,
Et, ecce, nunc in pulvere dormio.

VARIATION
ON A LINE BY BRYANT

In May, when sea-winds pierced our solitudes,
In the May winds not yet warmed out of malice,
At a certain doorway once I stood, my face
Leaning westward, a little before evening—
Oh, though all breath be seasonal, who can tell
A story like new grass blown in sunlight?

In May when winds blow westward into the light
As though both would depart our solitudes,
Though the door be different, what can I tell,
Feeling the sun thus fail from all life and malice?
But once the measure and sight of day, at evening,
Died in the shadows, so, of a cold face.

You that have forsaken the door, the face,
Burgeon, body, decrease, the turning light,
Who keep such single quiet both morning and evening
That approach but multiplies your solitudes,
Whether the bodily death is death to malice
Not the intrusions of sea-wind tell.

Let a kind diction out of the shadows tell,
Now toward my slumber, a legend unto my face
Of sleep as a quiet garden without malice
Where body moves, after the bitter light,
A staid dance among innocent solitudes;
So let me lie in a story, heavy with evening.

But I dream of distances where at evening
Ghost begins (as no migrant birds can tell)
A journey through outlandish solitudes,
Hair all ways lifted, leaves wild against face,
Feet trammeled among dune grass, with spent light,
And finds no roof at last against wind or malice.

Sir, who have locked your doors, but without malice,
Or madam, who draw your shawl against evening,
By the adumbrations of your thin light
What but this poor contention can you tell:
Ceaseless intruders have demeaned your face
And contrived homesteads in your solitudes.

Tell me who keeps infrangible solitudes
But the evening's dead on whose decided face
Morning repeats the malice and the light.

35

OVER THE BIER OF THE WORLDING

My friends, what can I say,
Having forgotten the feeling and the time
When it seemed that a dull body,
That even a dead man could dream
Those small belligerent birds, perhaps one gull,
Turning over the foul
Pond by the colliery,
These waters flicked by a regardless wind,
And the clouds, not of this country,
Sailing, as I had imagined;
Then these faces, even as I am, stilled,
Conforming to the world.
That which I kept, one body
And a few clothes, are brought to following
Processes as of poverty,
Suffering but not knowing,
Lying unimproved by the long season
And the falling rain.

EPITAPH
ON CERTAIN SCHISMATICS

These were they whom the body could not please,
Shaded between the shaded lights who rose
Quavering and forsook the arrogant knees,
The bodies death had made incredulous.
They had known, that season, lights in the trees
Moving when none felt wind, whisper of candles,
Pursuit of strange hinds, signs in snarled spindles,
Omens from alien birds, and after these
They descended into Hell. "Suffering is
Measure of nothing, now measure is lost," one said.
They fell to stroking their shyest histories.
Even cool flesh (so gaunt they grew and loveless),
When they could best remember it, only made
A wry shadow between the quick and the dead.

SUSPICOR
SPECULUM

TO SISYPHUS

Seeing, where the rock falls blind, this figure
At whispers swaying the drained countenance,
As might a shadow stand, I have stayed an hour
To no sound but his persistent sibilance,
Aghast, as should the populous dreaming head
See evils colder than the brain yet burn,
Or swift and tomorrow the enormous dead
Scatter their pose and, Sisyphus, return.
Patience betrays and the time speaks nothing. Come,
Pursed in the indigent small dark confess:
Is mine this shade that to all hours the same
Lurches and fails, marine and garrulous—
A vain myth in the winter of his sense,
Capable neither of song nor silence?

EPITAPH

Death is not information.
Stone that I am,
He came into my quiet
And I shall be still for him.

ODE:
THE MEDUSA FACE

When did I pass the pole where I deprived
Three hags of their one eye, then, staring, seized
The total of their dark
And took their answer?
For that way I came though the eye forgets:
Now tall over the breathless shore this day
Lifts on one equal glare
The crass and curling face.
I cannot tell if stone is upon me
Healing me, clotting time until I stand
Dead. If the heart yet moves,
What shield were faithful found,
What weapon? I stand as in sloth of stone,
Amazed, for a maimed piece of one's own death,
Should that lithe hair stiffen,
Were the shape of her fall.

40

FESTIVAL

Laughter is not celebration
And may not coax with renewal
The closed heads bending
In their garden at heal of evening.

I that am king of no country—
Shall a mind of dry leaves
On the erstwhile meadow
Invoke for me a gray retinue?

I would have a weather
Of spells and reflections
Whether dawn or a moon hang
In the green lagoon where fish swim.

You have seen the afternoon
Turn among shadows under
A flutter of paper and laurel.
Was that a dance or hesitancy?

And a body that made
A spectre his companion,
Fruitless until dark,
Lay down and embraced a lean shadow.

DICTUM:

FOR A MASQUE OF DELUGE

FOR DIDO

There will be the cough before the silence, then
Expectation; and the hush of portent
Must be welcomed by a diffident music
Lisping and dividing its renewals;
Shadows will lengthen and sway, and, casually
As in a latitude of diversion
Where growth is topiary, and the relaxed horizons
Are accustomed to the trespass of surprise,
One with a mask of Ignorance will appear
Musing on the wind's strange pregnancy.

And to him one must enter from the south
In a feigned haste, with disaster on his lips,
And tales of distended seas, continents
Submerged, worlds drowned, and of drownings
In mirrors; unto this foreboding
Let them add sidelong but increasing mention,
With darkening syllables, of shadows, as though
They stood and traded restlessness beneath
A gathering dark, until their figures seem
But a flutter of speech down an expense of wind.

So, with talk, like a blather of rain, begun,
Weather will break and the artful world will rush
Incontinent. There must be a vessel.
There must be rummage and shuffling for salvation
Till on that stage and violence, among
Curtains of tempest and shaking sea,
A covered basket, where a child might lie,
Timbered with osiers and floated on a shadow,
Glides adrift, as improbably sailing
As a lotus flower bearing a bull.

Hills are to be forgotten; the patter of speech
Must lilt upon flatness. The beasts will come;
And as they come, let one man, by the ark,
Drunken with desolation, his tongue
Rounding the full statement of the seasons,
Tremble and stare, his eyes seeming to chase
A final clatter of doomed crows, to seek
An affirmation, a mercy, an island,
Or hills crested with towns, and to find only
Cities of cloud already crumbling.

And these the beasts: the bull from the lotus flower
With wings at his shoulders; and a goat, winged;
A serpent undulating in the air;
A lion with wings like falling leaves;
These are to wheel on a winged wheel above
The sullen ark, while hare, swine, crocodile,
Camel and mouse come; and the sole man, always,
Lurches on childish limbs above the basket—
To his mere humanity seas shall not attain
With tempest, nor the obscure sky with torches.

(Why is it rumored that these beasts come in pairs
When the anatomies of their existence
Are wrought for singularity? They walk
Beside their shadows; their best motions are
Figments on the drapery of the air.
Their propagation is a redoubling
Merely of dark against the wall, a planetary
Leaning in the night unto their shadows
And stiffening to the moment of eclipse;
Shadows will be their lean progeny.)

At last the sigh of recession: the land
Wells from the water; the beasts depart; the man
Whose shocked speech must conjure a landscape
As of some country where the dead years keep
A circle of silence, a drying vista of ruin,
Musters himself, rises, and stumbling after
The dwindling beasts, under the all-colored
Paper rainbow, whose arc he sees as promise,
Moves in an amazement of resurrection,
Solitary, impoverished, renewed.

A falling frond may seem all trees. If so
We know the tone of falling. We shall find
Dictions for rising, words for departure;
And time will be sufficient before that revel
To teach an order and rehearse the days
Till the days are accomplished: so now the dove
Makes assignations with the olive tree,
Slurs with her voice the gestures of the time:
The day foundering, the dropping sun
Heavy, the wind a low portent of rain.

THE BONES OF PALINURUS
PRAY TO THE NORTH STAR

Console us. The wind chooses among us.
Our whiteness is a night wake disordered.
Lone candor, be constant over
Us desolate who gleam no direction.

SESTINA

FOR ROBERT GRAVES

Where I came by torchlight there is dawn-song:
Leaves remembering, sudden as a name
Recalled from nowhere, remembering morning,
Fresh wind in high grass, cricket on plowshare,
Whisper of stream in the green-shadowed place,
Thrush and tanager keeping season.

Have I not also willed to be heard in season?
Have I not heard anger raised in a song
And watched when many went out to a wild place
And fought with the dark to make themselves a name?
I have seen of those champions how thin a share
After one night shook off their sleep at morning.

In a stony month a long cloud darkened morning.
Their feet gone white, shuffling the cold season,
The breath of some was worn too small to share.
Have I not heard how fragile then grew song?
Gray water lashed at the island of one's name.
And some stayed to flutter empty in that place.

48

What road is it one follows out of that place?
I remember no direction. I dreamed of morning,
Walking, warming the tongue over a name.
And a few of us came out of that season
As though from sleep, and stood too bleak for song,
And saw hills and heaven in the one dawn share.

Whom shall I praise before the gray knife share?
I have gone like seed into a dark place.
Whom shall I choose to make new with song?
For there will be sinking between night and morning,
Lisp of hushed voices, a dwindled season,
The small lights that flicker at a name.

Where again shall I walk with various name?
Merciless restlessness falls to my share.
Whose house shall I fill for more than a season?
I woke with new words, and in every place,
Under different lights, evening and morning,
Under many masters studied one song.

A breathed name I was with no resting-place,
A bough of sleep that had no share of morning,
Till I had made body and season from a song.

HERONS

As I was dreaming between hills
That stones wake in a changing land,
There in the country of morning
I slept, and the hour and shadow slept.

I became the quiet stone
By a river where the winds
Favor honest thoughts. Three herons
Rose into a hemlock tree.

And I heard, "All day I stand
Dreaming that the night has come;
Beneath my wings, beneath my feet
The resignation and the death."

And, "When will darkness bury me
Who stand all day with open eye,
The small eye through which the years pass
From one place to another place."

And, "I have neither eye nor dream;
Dumb as with sleep or dignity
I stand, and others speak of me
In questions, but no prophecy."

But I knew neither dream nor eye
And held my question till a wind
Shook them in their hemlock tree
And I became the man who fell

After the lightning long ago
At his own window; there he stood
And leaned out on the afternoon
Till someone touched him, and he fell.

Daylong I dreamed as one who sets
His impudence in a falling house
And laughs and sleeps. The ruined hour
Moves and outmodes this comedy.

Who will see me if I fall?
I waked between the quiet hills;
I saw the dark and came away
And night where I had lain all day.

SONG
WITH THE EYES CLOSED

I am the shape in sleep
While the seasonal beasts
With petulant rough step
Forsake my random coasts.

I am the face recedes
Though the pool be constant
Whose double kingdom feeds
The sole vein's discontent.

I have seen desire, such
As a violent hand,
Murder my sleep—as much
Is suffered of the wind.

CANCIÓN Y GLOSA

Y yo, mientras, hijo
tuyo, con más secas
hojas en las venas.
                    —Jiménez

Among the almond trees
whiteness more than winter's,
speech where no name is,
flowers broken from sleep;
and you their litany,
a breath upon this fervor,
you their reason, lady,
seem as a name, meanwhile,
for an immortal season,
who stand in such whiteness
with these green leaves in your hands.

There is no breath of days
in that time where I was,
in that place, through the trees;
no winds nor satellites,
seasons nor bodies rise;
are no descent of rivers,
wavering of fishes,
indecision of tides,
langor before pause,
nor any dance to please,
nor prayers, pleasure of knees,
coupling, smile of increase,
swaying of fruit and seas,
genesis, exodus,
tremor of arteries,
decay by calendars,
hum of carrion flies;
and no shadow-plays,
trepidation of fingers,
ruse of limbs or faces
ghosts nor histories
shift before the eyes,
but that vain country lies
in savorless repose.

Among the names of these,
yet as the eyes remove
now from the polities
of these disstated things,
I their artifice,
a breath among such langor,
I their name, lady,
seem as one nameless, leaning
through such stillness meanwhile
with these dry leaves in my hands.

CAROL

On vague hills the prophet bird
Chants now the night is drained;
What was the stem this night stirred
And root from the winter ground?

Lord, Lord, and no night remained,
But heaven only, whence comes
Light such as no sun contained,
And the earth shook, and our limbs.

By song we were brought to stand
By that flower where frail our eyes
Strayed among beasts and found
Dim kings dreaming on their knees.

Lord, Lord, and earth's hours were torn
To dreams and we beheld there
On that silence newly born
Heaven's light in the still flower.

From such a quiet wakened,
After the vision has burned
On such birth, to what end
Have dew and hours returned?

Lord, Lord, and what remember
We of dreams when the day comes,
And the loud bird laughs on wonder
And white sheep lying like tombs?

We who are flesh have no word
And distraction is our music,
Who on the anxious night heard
Peace over our voices break.

CAROL OF
THE THREE KINGS

How long ago we dreamed
Evening and the human
Step in the quiet groves
And the prayer we said:
Walk upon the darkness,
Words of the lord,
Contain the night, the dead
And here comfort us.
We have been a shadow
Many nights moving,
Swaying many nights
Between yes and no.
We have been blindness
Between sun and moon
Coaxing the time
For a doubtful star.
Now we cease, we forget
Our reasons, our city,
The sun, the perplexed day,

Noon, the irksome labor,
The flushed dream, the way,
Even the dark beasts,
Even our shadows.
In this night and day
All gifts are nothing:
What is frankincense
Where all sweetness is?
We that were followers
In the night's confusion
Kneel and forget our feet
Who the cold way came.
Now in the darkness
After the deep song
Walk among the branches
Angels of the lord,
Over earth and child
Quiet the boughs.
Now shall we sing or pray?
Where has the night gone?
Who remembers day?
We are breath and human
And awake have seen
All birth and burial
Merge and fall away,
Seen heaven that extends
To comfort all the night,
We have felt morning move
The grove of a few hands.

CAROL

Lady, the dew of years
Makes sodden the world
And yet there is no morning.
Lady, we cannot think you
Indifferent or far,
And we lean and call after
You who in the night,
As a morning, among
This our heaviness came
And our eyes called you maiden.
We are in the darkness,
Our eyes turned to the door,
Waiting. Because you passed
Through the room where we are,
Your form not cumbered
With our weight and gesture;
Waiting, because you went
Uncontained by our shadows,
As a light, quietly;
Leaning, as though you might
Come again where our eyes
Are lost that follow after
You who as a light
Through the room where we are
With grace carried a flower.

A POEM
FOR DOROTHY

No shape in darkness single stands
And we in privacy and night,
Taking surprise of love for light,
Merged the dark fortunes of our hands.

Patience of fire insists and warms
Through dust, through dusty bone the breath;
The ear and intellect of death
Direct of love the heated forms.

Sitting on stones we kiss to please
Some stilled remembrance that shares our blood,
And warmth whose shape and name were dead
From ruin moving amends our peace.

HERMIONE ON SIMULACRA

FOR DIANA WYNYARD

(Paulina draws back a curtain and
discovers Hermione as a statue.)

For comfort I became a stone,
Silent where whispers stir,
I who had longed to be immune
To all tongues that infest the air.

I schooled the body where it dreamed,
I hushed all offices till I
Quiet and blind as Justice seemed
And I reigned in a still kingdom.

I banished motion, but have found
No simplicity in stone,
For one comes who believes and bends
Before me and makes me many things.

As one who stares and seems a prey
To the darkness of premonitions,
So in a fantasy he comes
And finds it already night.

He is a vagrant in my shadow,
An alien darkness, how should he know
I have conspired to this deathly
Dancing to unmoving music?

Both cause and image I became;
I am his innocence who grieves,
And while he tells all he believes
I of us both the mirror am.

I am the patience of a pool
Where all the planets sway, and I
Am the moon's self, a watery star
Beheld at night in a blue river.

I am the night where he is blind
And I the orbit of his prayers;
Quiet above the suppliant hand,
I am the heaven of fixed stars.

I the elusive phoenix seem,
And a man is my age and fire,
For he has breathed me to this flame,
And I, seeming myself, seem fire.

Thus I who have not moved a limb,
Who feigned but changelessness and keep
Only the semblance that I was
Am all faces of time and sleep.

I had intended but to be
My picture in a stone, but I
Took shape of death and have become
Death, and all things come to me.

Death, in my varied majesty
I am astonished in flesh and stone
That you should be simplicity
Whose visage so resembles me.

SONG

How have I dreamed you, Lady,
Stricken among flames dark auburn:
O Lady, does your chimney burn?
Winds are moving dangerously;
I may be slow to warn;
Give me tidings in my concern:
O Lady, Lady, does your chimney burn?

If it would please you, Lady,
I could make your defences stubborn
Against odd wind and conflagration;
Or if flame owns you utterly
I might assure return
Better than ashes in your urn.
O Lady, Lady, does your chimney burn?

Or do you lack, Lady,
An intimate subaltern,
A tall sentry near your postern?
I shall fulfill as you employ me,
Turn as you bid me turn,
And be pleased if you so govern.
O Lady, Lady, does your chimney burn?

Or if I might be sea
To your green island laced with fern,
I should betide your coasts in turn
Learning your seasons, and so be
Fierce, as you pleased, or southern,
Wearing the air that you had worn.
O Lady, Lady, does your chimney burn?

Even, for your pleasure, Lady,
I could become your heat and learn
To rise for you when your mood is eastern,
And I should by such service, surely,
More than bare praises earn,
And all I received of you return;
O Lady, Lady, does your chimney burn?

SONG

Mirrors we lay wherein desire
Traded, by dark, conceits of fire;
As gardened minds whose delicacy
Could neither close with flesh nor flee,

Who watched by fire a bush inflect
What flame a window could reflect
Where dark and distance were control
So the leaves burned yet rested whole;

But flesh, dark forest to the mind,
Took at our breaths repeated wind
And from our eyes an equal glare:
Our distance broke and burned us there.

In married dark these fevers learn
Alternate loss; the bodies, worn
Indefinite, attend together
Night's pleasure and the press of weather.